NI S

Hazel Edwards
illustrated by Anne-Maree Lyons

GINN

GINN

1996 UK edition published by Ginn and Company Limited
Prebendal House, Parson's Fee, Aylesbury, Bucks HP20 2QY
ISBN 0 602 26998 9

Printed in Hong Kong by Dah Hua Printing Press Co., Ltd.

CONTENTS

1

Wear-a-lot

Have you heard about “Nibbles”? They are the clothes you can eat. They were made by Toula.

It all started at the Wear-a-lot Shop.

"What can we do? Nobody wants to buy our clothes," said Toula. She tidied the clothes because there were no customers.

"We're going broke," said Judi, the manager.

Business was bad. In the Parkwhere Shopping Centre, thirteen other shops sold clothes too. But no-one was buying.

"What can we do?" said Judi.

"I'll think of something," said Toula. "Wear-a-lot" was Toula's first job. If the shop closed down, she wouldn't *have* a job.

"Our clothes must be different. And we'll have to get people to visit our shop. Being at the back of the shopping centre is a problem," said Toula.

"How will we get people to come?" asked Judi.

"I don't know ... yet."

There was a smell of hot bread from the bakery. That gave Toula her first idea.

"Let's make clothes to eat."

"How?" said Judi.

"Let's make clothes out of food." said Toula. "Customers will eat them. Then they'll come back for more."

So they designed some food clothes. Bread-roll jumpers. Lettuce skirts. Carrot ring T-shirts. Banana skin shoes. Peanut earrings.

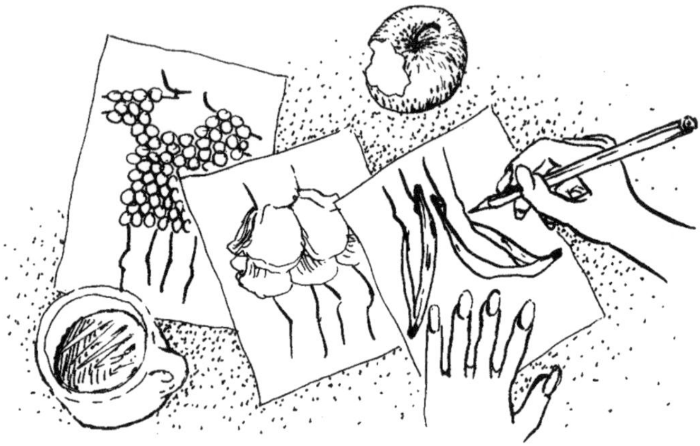

"Clothes made from food!" said Judi. "No-one else would think of that!"

2

Bread creations

At five o'clock on Monday morning, Toula was at "Bready", the hot bread shop. The cooks were making their rolls, bagels and buns. Toula was very busy. She joined and cut and stuck bread together. By nine o'clock she had made ten sets of clothes. Carefully, she carried them into "Wear-a-lot".

"Aren't you clever!" cried Judi in admiration.

Judi tried on the bread clothes. Then she had a nibble. "Wonderful. Very tasty."

Toula nodded. "Today we will sell our Bread Creations."

A microphone was borrowed. Toula changed into the "bready" clothes. She had a practice nibble.

"Tastes great!"

"If the customers nibble too much, they'll be naked," warned Judi.

"That's okay." Toula smiled. "After they nibble one set of clothes, they'll come back for more."

"Look Mummy! She's wearing bread!" A little boy yelled.

Toula smiled as the boy's mother came closer.

"Is that a croissant?" asked the mother. "Croissants are my favourite Saturday breakfast."

"Yes," nodded Toula. Her shirt was made from croissants. Her jeans were slices of bread stuck with honey. On her feet were bread-roll sneakers with poppy seeds.

"My cream cake earrings wouldn't stay on. I'll try party pies tomorrow."

"Or sausage rolls," said Judi, who was looking happier now. The shop was crowded. Customers heard Toula on the microphone. Everybody wanted to try on the food clothes.

Toula showed the Bagel Bikini. Then she wore the French Stick Coat. But the Sliced Bread Mini-skirt was the most popular.

"This mini-skirt is for playing squash or tennis. Don't sweat too much. The bread gets soggy," warned Toula. "And then it tastes salty."

Everybody laughed.

Judi sewed a label into each creation.

Soon customers started to line up outside "Wear-a-lot."

"I'll have one of the honey bread skirts."

"Could I have one stuck with apricot jam?"

"I'd like strawberry."

Judi smiled. The cash register pinged all morning.

"Nibble while you wear." Toula said to the crowds. "Snack on your sleeve. Bite on your blouse. Taste your T-shirt."

3

New ideas to eat

"Do you have a weight-watcher's dress?" asked a voice from the back.

Toula looked up quickly. "Call in on Wednesday. We'll have our Diet Clothes then."

"What Diet Clothes?" hissed Judi. "We haven't got any."

"We will have," smiled Toula. "I'll speak to Ross."

Ross was from the "Fruity Fruit Palace". He was happy to help. Toula's customers went past his shop too. He needed more trade.

At "Bready" the bakery business was good now.

On Wednesday, customers loved Toula's fruit and vegetable clothes. Melon slice skirts. Banana belts. Lettuce leaf tops. Peach and pear T-shirts. A pullover of spinach, cabbage and other greens was popular. Weight-watchers liked it best.

Celery stalk sandals and passionfruit pyjamas were for midnight snacks. They sold well.

But the jewellery was Judi's idea. She made earrings from mixed nuts. She made mushroom brooches. Then she made celery and carrot ring necklaces.

"Nine carat jewellery!" she laughed. A carat is a gold measure.

Toula smiled.

They made watchbands from strips of capsicum. Red watch bands to go with red clothes. Green watch bands to go with green clothes.

But then things went wrong!

4

Problems!

Toffee pyjamas stuck to the bed!

Cream puff shoes leaked.

Pizza jumpers were smelly.

Imagine sitting in a squashy melon skirt.

Suntanned swimmers complained. Their tomato bikinis grilled in the hot sun. The pineapple peel shirts had prickles. They left a rash.

Then there was a problem with the "Melting Moments" ice-cream clothes.

"Will it be hot today?" Toula looked up at the sky.

"Yes." said Judi. "Thirty degrees."

"Oh, no!" said Toula.

"I want my money back!" The big woman dripped sticky white goo on the floor.

"When I went into the sun, my ice-cream shirt melted! And I didn't even have a nibble!" she protested.

"Look at the label," said Judi.
It said:

"We did tell you to hang it in the freezer, when you weren't wearing it." said Toula.

But they gave the woman her money back.

5

What next?

The “Melting Moments” were like their name.

“Just one lick and they’re gone,” yawned Toula. She was so tired.

Every morning she went to the market at four o’clock with Ross.

She chose the best fruit to make her Eat Today Jewellery.

Berry earrings were best-sellers. Strawberry. Blueberry. Raspberry. The blackberry ones left stains on the ears.

"Just stand in the rain for a few minutes," said Toula. "That'll wash your ears."

But the customers didn't like black ears.

At first, Toula made ONE DAY EAT AND WEAR Clothes. Then she made the longer THREE DAY food clothes.

Customers loved them.

"Keep your T-shirt in the fridge overnight. It will still be fresh in the morning," said Toula.

At five o'clock in the morning, she helped in the bakery.

She made new bready shapes.

At six o'clock, she started to stick, honey or jam her clothes together.

Each day, a shopful of clothes had to be ready by nine o'clock.

6

Waiting in line

Faces pushed against the window. They hoped to taste a new fashion.

Often the customers shivered. They had nibbled most of yesterday's clothes.

Keeping up the supply of clothes was not the only problem.

"Look what you've done to me!" Stan from the furniture store stormed into the shop. "Nobody wants to buy our wardrobes any more. They keep their clothes in the fridge or in their tummies," he complained.

"It's all your fault! Ever since you started selling food clothes, people don't come to our shop. I'm going to complain to the manager of the shopping centre."

"I'm sorry," said Judi. "But 'Bready' and Ross are very happy. They have many new customers."

"Advertise your wardrobes as Food Clothes Storers," suggested Toula with a yawn. She didn't mean to be rude. She was just tired. She wanted to sleep in pyjamas not made of squashy fruit.

"Hadn't thought of advertising like that," said Stan.

So Toula gave him an orange peel earring.

"Er. Thanks."

"You're welcome."

Meanwhile the signwriter painted "Nibbles" on the window. The new name came from Judi.

"Perhaps this is the beginning of a chain of 'Nibbles' shops?" Judi said.

STAN'S FURNITURE

Toula wasn't sure. She longed to wear her faded denim jeans again. Banana peel jeans usually split when she bent over.

7

Specials!

Every day, Toula wrote a “use by” date on the inside of each outfit.

“Here are the One Day Specials. Then the Two Day and the Three Day. After that, you’ll need new ones.”

Judi put the clothes on the cool rack. Then she switched on the fan. She sprayed the fruit skirts with water to keep them fresh.

"More like running a plant nursery than a clothes shop," said Judi.

Soon, the customers started to complain.

"I want a dress to last more than one day."

"Haven't you any Last-a-Week outfits?"

That's when Toula decided on her plan. She whispered her idea to Judi, who nodded. Next morning, there was a big sign in front of the shop.

Overnight, the signwriter had painted a "No" in front of the "Nibbles" sign.

"We have a new range of Wear-a-Lot clothes." said Toula.

The crowd gathered around.

"The clothes are made from wool and cotton. You don't have to eat them. You can use them one day, wash and wear the next," said Judi.

"Just what we wanted." The customers rushed the "No Nibbles" clothes racks.

Next month, Judi and Toula have agreed, they might try Smelly Jewellery. But not onion rings!